Who Was Mister Rogers?

by Diane Bailey

illustrated by Dede Putra

Penguin Workshop

For A.J. and Evan, who make the days special—DB

Dedicated to my little dragon, Ryu—DP

PENGUIN WORKSHOP
An Imprint of Penguin Random House LLC, New York

If you purchased this book without a cover, you should be aware that this book is stolen property. It was reported as "unsold and destroyed" to the publisher, and neither the author nor the publisher has received any payment for this "stripped book."

Penguin supports copyright. Copyright fuels creativity, encourages diverse voices, promotes free speech, and creates a vibrant culture. Thank you for buying an authorized edition of this book and for complying with copyright laws by not reproducing, scanning, or distributing any part of it in any form without permission. You are supporting writers and allowing Penguin to continue to publish books for every reader.

The publisher does not have any control over and does not assume any responsibility for author or third-party websites or their content.

Copyright © 2019 by Penguin Random House LLC. All rights reserved. Published by Penguin Workshop, an imprint of Penguin Random House LLC, New York. PENGUIN and PENGUIN WORKSHOP are trademarks of Penguin Books Ltd. WHO HQ & Design is a registered trademark of Penguin Random House LLC. Printed in the USA.

Visit us online at www.penguinrandomhouse.com.

Library of Congress Cataloging-in-Publication Data is available upon request.

ISBN 9781524792190 (paperback)   10 9 8 7 6 5 4 3 2 1
ISBN 9781524792206 (library binding)   10 9 8 7 6 5 4 3 2 1

Contents

Who Was Mister Rogers?

One day when Fred Rogers was in high school, his teacher asked him for a favor. Another boy, Jim Stumbaugh, had gotten seriously hurt during football practice. He'd be in the hospital for a while. He was well enough to keep up with his homework, though—if Fred would take his books to him.

Fred hesitated. He and Jim didn't know each other well. Jim was a popular athlete. He was a star on the football team, the basketball team, and the track team. He got straight As. He succeeded at everything, and everyone liked him. Fred was not at all like Jim. He wasn't athletic or outgoing.

Fred wanted to help out, though. So he agreed to visit Jim in the hospital. Fred was surprised at how well they got along. Jim was more than a good athlete—he was a good person. Jim and Fred became friends.

When Jim came back to school, he spread the word: "That Rogers kid's okay." Fred's friendship with Jim helped him become more confident and outgoing, and Fred was always grateful to him. Jim had shown Fred how one person can change someone's life.

Years later, Fred did the same thing. He created and starred in his own children's television program, *Mister Rogers' Neighborhood*. Fred used the program to help kids understand they were special just by being themselves. They were always welcome in Fred's world, just like Jim Stumbaugh had made Fred welcome in his.

CHAPTER 1
A Shy Boy

Fred Rogers was born on March 20, 1928, into a wealthy family in Latrobe, Pennsylvania, not far from the city of Pittsburgh. His father, James, owned a factory that made bricks for furnaces. His mother, Nancy, took care of the family.

They were loving and attentive parents, and they taught Fred to be kind to other people. Nancy volunteered at the local hospital and knitted sweaters for soldiers. James would leave pennies on people's windowsills. He liked to imagine their faces when they found them.

The Great Depression

The Great Depression began in 1929. After the stock market crashed on October 29 of that year, many businesses were ruined. Ordinary people lost their homes and life savings when banks were forced to close. By 1933, a few short years later, one in every four Americans was out of work.

The Great Depression lasted for ten years and was one of the worst financial disasters in modern history.

Near the end of the Depression, when Fred was eleven, his parents adopted a baby girl, Nancy Elaine. (They called her "Laney.") Until Laney came along, though, Fred was an only child. Without a brother or sister, he was always looking for ways to have fun by himself.

To make up for not having many real-life friends, he created pretend ones. He used paper bags or old socks to make puppets. He gave them different names and voices, and they all had their own personalities. As long as Fred had his puppets, he didn't get too lonely. He always had someone to talk to!

He also "talked" through his music. He loved to play songs on the piano to express himself. "I was always able to cry or laugh or say I was angry through the tips of my fingers on the piano," he said.

He had begun playing the piano when he was five. A few years later, his grandmother offered to buy him a piano. She said he could pick out whichever one he wanted. Fred chose a grand piano. It was one of the fanciest, most expensive pianos in the store. His grandmother had not expected to spend that much money! But she'd made Fred a promise, and she kept it.

Fred sometimes had trouble fitting in with other kids. He was shy and chubby, and he got sick a lot. He had terrible allergies, and if there was a cold going around, Fred always seemed to catch it! Sometimes his mother wouldn't even let him leave the house. Fred was stuck indoors while everyone else was outside playing.

His family was wealthier than most people in Latrobe, and some kids were annoyed by that. The Rogerses even hired a driver to take Fred to school each day. Sometimes Fred asked the driver to drop him off a block away so he could walk up to the building with everyone else. But he still knew he was different.

Fred did have a good friend in George Allen. George was an African American boy whose mother had worked as a housekeeper for the Rogers family. After she died, Fred's mother invited George to live with their family. George was quite a bit older than Fred, and Fred looked up to him like a big brother. In those days it wasn't common for white people to be friends with black people, but Fred didn't care. He saw George as his friend, no matter what other people thought.

CHAPTER 2
Early Lessons

One day when Fred was eight, his school let out early, and the family driver could not pick Fred up. He started to walk home by himself. Soon Fred noticed a group of boys following him. They made him nervous, and he walked faster. Then they began calling out insults. "Hey, Fat Freddy!"

they yelled. "We're going to get you!" Frightened, Fred ran to the house of a neighbor. She let him come inside and stay until the boys left.

When Fred's parents found out what happened, they told Fred not to worry about it. If he acted like he didn't care what the boys said, they'd leave him alone. The problem was, Fred *did* care. His feelings were hurt. He didn't understand why those boys were so mean.

There was one person Fred knew he could always count on, though: Ding Dong. That was his grandfather. The nickname came from a nursery rhyme his grandfather sang to him.

Fred's grandfather Fred
Brooks McFeely (Ding Dong)

Ding Dong always knew how to make Fred feel good, and Fred loved spending time at his grandparents' farm on the weekends. At home, he often had to sit inside quietly. His mother's tidy home was not to be messed up! But at the farm, there was plenty of room to run around and explore. One thing Fred wanted to do was climb the stone walls that wound all over the farm. He knew his mother wouldn't let him, though. The walls were old and falling to pieces. He might hurt himself! Sure enough, when he asked her for permission one day, the answer was no.

Then his grandfather spoke up. "Let the boy climb the stone walls," he said. "He has to learn to do things for himself." Fred was thrilled that his grandfather trusted him. He spent the next couple of hours climbing the walls. At the end of the day, Ding Dong told Fred, "Freddy, you made the day special just by being yourself."

For a boy who did not have much self-confidence, it was an important thing to hear. Fred never forgot those words.

George Allen continued to be a big part of
Fred's life and shared many of his interests with
him. George taught Fred about photography,
and Fred discovered he liked to take pictures—
especially ones with people in them. George also
introduced Fred to jazz. Fred loved how the music
sounded. It was full of surprises.

Another of George's passions was flying. In the 1940s, George helped train a group of African American pilots who attended Tuskegee Institute in Alabama. The Tuskegee Airmen, as they became known, were an important part of the American forces during World War II. When Fred reached high school, George taught him to fly a small plane. George's enthusiasm rubbed off on Fred.

A plane used by the Tuskegee Airmen

"The best teacher in the world is somebody who loves what he or she does, and just loves it in front of you," Fred used to say. For a while, Fred wanted to be a pilot, too!

In high school, Fred still felt like he was chubby and weak, so he saved up nineteen dollars and sent away for a mail-order exercise program. Then he did all the workouts. But they didn't work. Fred realized he was never going to look like a bodybuilder. He was just going to have to be himself.

Fred found the things he was good at and concentrated on them. He joined the French club and the photography club. He edited the yearbook and wrote for the school newspaper. He was elected president of the student council.

He had finally found his place.

CHAPTER 3
Leaving Home

Fred graduated from high school in 1946. By then he'd changed his mind about becoming a pilot. Instead, he decided to become a diplomat, someone who works with people from other countries to help solve problems. He enrolled at Dartmouth College in Hanover, New Hampshire. He planned to study foreign languages like French and Italian.  They would help him talk to people from different parts of the world.

After a year, though, Fred decided he didn't like Dartmouth very much. The winters were long and cold. He thought the teachers weren't very friendly. Plus, he missed making music. Fred transferred into the music department at Rollins College in Winter Park, Florida. He liked the people at Rollins College—and the warmer weather was nice, too!

One of the first people Fred met was another music student named Joanne Byrd. She was amazed by how Fred could play the piano "by ear"—without using any sheet music. Sometimes he played popular songs everyone knew. Other times he could make one up on the spot. No one else could do that! The two became good friends.

At Rollins, Fred was a good student. In 1951, he was set to graduate with a degree in music. Then he wanted to continue his education at a seminary, a place where he would study to become a minister. Fred had grown up going to church, and he wanted religion to be an important part of his life.

But everything changed during his last year of college.

When he came home for a school break, his parents had a surprise to show him: They'd bought a television! Television was still very new in the early 1950s, and not many families owned one. Fred had never watched TV. He was curious to see it.

Later, Fred could not remember the name of the first program he watched, but he did remember one thing: It was terrible! It showed people throwing pies in each other's faces. Fred thought it was just a silly waste of time.

TV was coming into more living rooms every day. If the programs were made well, television could be both entertaining and educational. It could be a wonderful way to reach people, especially young people.

The Early Days of Television

One of the first television stations to begin broadcasting was from a General Electric plant in New York State in 1928. But not too many people saw the news program that WRGB aired three days a week. Almost no one owned a television set yet!

By 1951, there were about ten million sets in the United States. Everything was still broadcast in black and white, and stations did not broadcast overnight. But audiences loved all the entertainment they could watch without having to leave their homes! Most shows were broadcast live, meaning that audiences saw them at the same time they were being performed in the studio.

By the mid-1960s, color television sets began outselling black-and-white ones.

31

After watching a single show, Fred made a big decision. He told his parents that he wasn't going to the seminary after all. Instead, he was going to look for a job in the television business.

They were surprised—and not sure Fred had thought things through.

"You've never even seen it!" they told him.

"Well, I've seen enough of it here that I'd like to try!" replied Fred.

He knew he was doing the right thing.

CHAPTER 4
In the Studio

After he graduated college in 1951, Fred moved to New York City, where he applied for a job at NBC. The television network needed an assistant producer to work on several of its music programs, and Fred had a degree in music. That was a good fit, and he was hired. Although the job sounded important, at first Fred mostly served coffee and ran errands. He learned how to deal with many different kinds of people. Once, he was yelled at for bringing someone the wrong drink! Fred remembered that feeling. He might never be famous or important, but he would always try to treat people well.

Before long, Fred got promoted to the job of floor manager. He worked on several programs,

like *NBC Opera Theatre*, *The Kate Smith Hour*, *The Gabby Hayes Show*, and *Your Hit Parade*. As floor manager, Fred's job was to make sure everything ran smoothly. He was in charge of telling the crew—the people who worked behind the scenes—when to change the sets. He got the props the actors needed.

Sometimes he needed a little help to get "the red vase" or "the green parrot." Fred was color-blind, so he could not tell red from green!

Fred Rogers on the set of *The Gabby Hayes Show*

He also gave actors their cues to get on or off the stage. He was always looking at the clock, because everything was carefully timed. Since the shows aired live, there were no do-overs. Everyone had only one chance to get it right!

Of course, that didn't always happen. One time, Kate Smith was singing in front of a set painted to look like a farmhouse. When Fred thought the song was over, he told the crew to raise the set into the rafters over the stage. But he was too early! Kate wasn't finished yet.

As the set went up, it looked to the audience like she was sinking lower and lower! Everyone knew there would be mistakes from time to time, though. Most people laughed about them.

Fred also worked with the Western star Gabby Hayes, who had a show for children. Fred loved kids, and the two became friends. Television stars performed for thousands of people—and they couldn't even see them! Fred thought that must be hard. He asked Hayes how he did it. Hayes told him his secret. "Freddy," he said, "I think of one little buckaroo." He meant that he performed as if there were only one child in the audience. That made sense to Fred. People watching a movie or a play sat in an audience with a lot of other people. But when they watched TV, they did it in their homes. It was much more personal, like the show was playing just for them. Later, when Fred got in front of the camera himself, he always imagined talking to just "one little buckaroo."

Gabby Hayes (1885–1969)

Before he went into television, George "Gabby" Hayes was a popular movie actor who appeared in Western films in the 1930s and 1940s. The nickname "Gabby" came from a character that was created for him, Gabby Whittaker. In Hayes's movies, the star was usually a famous actor like Roy Rogers or John Wayne. Hayes usually played the loyal sidekick, who was often cranky but still a good-hearted friend. He was known for his funny expressions, such as "Yer durn tootin'!" and "Jumpin' Jehoshaphat!"

Fred had made new friends in New York, but he missed Joanne Byrd, his friend from college. She was still in Florida. Fred knew he wanted to spend the rest of his life with her. He wrote her a letter asking her to marry him. Joanne was so excited that she called him on the phone and accepted his proposal. They were married in 1952.

Fred's career was going great. He was on his way up the ladder. Then, yet again, Fred decided to make a sudden change.

CHAPTER 5
The Children's Corner

Fred liked working as a floor manager at NBC, but he didn't think it was quite the right job for him. He dreamed of making music and creating television programs himself, not just managing what *other* people created.

He heard that a new TV station, WQED, was starting up in Pittsburgh. Fred liked the idea of being near his hometown. Even more, he liked the idea that WQED was an educational station. WQED was operated by National Educational Television (NET), which became the Public Broadcasting Service (PBS) in 1970.

As an educational station, WQED was created to serve many different viewers. There would be room for all kinds of shows—not just the pie-in-the-face kind!

Fred's friends thought his plan was crazy. He already had a successful career in New York, and WQED wasn't even on the air yet! But Fred knew what he wanted. He and Joanne left New York for Pittsburgh in the fall of 1953. Fred was one of only six people hired at the new station. His job was to put together a schedule of programs.

The station manager, Dorothy Daniel, thought some of WQED's programming should be for children. Fred volunteered for the job. This would give him a chance to create a new TV show, just like he'd always wanted. He teamed up with Josie Carey, who also worked at the station, to make an hour a day of children's programming. Their budget was only thirty dollars per show, so they had to do something cheap!

They came up with the idea of a program called *The Children's Corner*. Josie would sing songs while Fred played the piano. In between, they would show short films.

Josie Carey

Commercial vs. Public Television

It can be quite expensive to make television shows. In commercial television, advertisers buy small chunks of airtime, during which they put on commercials for their products. The TV station then uses money earned from commercials to create TV programs. Commercial stations air shows that they think will be popular. When more people watch, the station can charge more money for commercials!

Public television stations do not air commercials. They make shows with money they get from the government,  as well as donations from people and companies. Public television stations don't have to worry about what the most popular kinds of shows might be. They often take chances on a wider variety of programs.

WQED started its regular programming on April 5, 1954. The night before, Dorothy Daniel threw a party for the staff. Everyone got a small gift. Fred's was a puppet that looked like a tiger. That was a perfect gift for him, since he had loved to play with puppets as a child. He named it Daniel Striped Tiger, after Dorothy Daniel.

The puppet gave Fred an idea. Why not use him on *The Children's Corner*? Part of the show's set was painted to look like a clock, and Fred cut a hole in the clock so Daniel could poke through from behind. Fred used a high, squeaky voice to make Daniel "talk" to Josie, who was in front of the set. The striped tiger was a hit! More puppets—and more voices by Fred—joined the cast later.

Putting on a live TV show kept everyone on their toes. As soon as Fred finished playing the piano for one scene, he had to dash across the stage to perform with the puppets. He started wearing sneakers at work so his footsteps would be quieter.

He also kept his hands in his pockets to stop his change from jingling as he ran!

Offstage, Fred's family was growing. He and Joanne had their first son, James, in 1959. Their second son, John, was born in 1961.

Being a father gave Fred firsthand experience with kids, but he wanted to know even more. He was interested in learning about young children's feelings. He wanted to understand why they thought and acted the way they did. He took classes in child development at the University of Pittsburgh and paid close attention to how children behaved.

Fred had also not forgotten about his goal of becoming a minister. He enrolled at Western Theological Seminary in Pittsburgh and took classes during his lunch hour. He finished school there in 1962.

By then Fred had been at WQED for almost ten years. Then, one day, he got an important call. It was from the director of children's programming for a TV station in Canada. The director wanted Fred to move to Canada to create an entirely new show for preschool children. Fred thought it was a great opportunity. He said yes.

CHAPTER 6
Welcome to the Neighborhood

When Fred arrived in Canada, he got a surprise: The programming director knew Fred personally. He'd seen him talk to children, and he thought Fred was great at it. So he wanted Fred to appear on the show, not just work the puppets offstage. Fred had never performed on camera,

but he agreed to try. The new show would even be named after him. It was called *Misterogers*.

The program was similar to *The Children's Corner*, with lots of music and a cast of puppets. It was a success, but after about a year, Fred was ready to come home. James and John would be starting school soon, and he and Joanne wanted to settle in Pittsburgh.

Joanne was busy with their sons, but when she had time she played piano concerts and gave lessons. Fred went back to WQED, where he turned *Misterogers* into *Misterogers' Neighborhood*. The new program went on the air in Pittsburgh in 1966, and it was quickly picked up to be shown on other stations. In 1967, Fred made a publicity appearance at a television station in Boston, Massachusetts. The organizers thought a few hundred people might come. They were shocked when thousands lined up around the block to meet Mister Rogers!

By 1968, Fred split the title *Misterogers* into two words, and *Mister Rogers' Neighborhood* was airing all over the country. The first season was in black and white, but for the second season, Fred started taping the program in color.

Each show began with a song Fred had written himself, "Won't You Be My Neighbor?" Fred sang:

I have always wanted to have a neighbor just like you . . .

Would you be mine?

Could you be mine?

Won't you be my neighbor?

The answer was a big *yes*! *Mister Rogers' Neighborhood* was becoming one of the most popular programs on public television.

The program actually had two neighborhoods. One was very realistic. There, Mister Rogers lived in a comfortable home where friends could stop by to chat. There was also a pretend world, a royal kingdom called the "Neighborhood of Make-Believe." The puppets lived there. A red toy trolley traveled between Mister Rogers's living room and the castle in Make-Believe. When kids heard the trolley bell ring, they knew they were leaving one neighborhood and going to the other.

Fred paid attention to every detail of the show. He wrote all the episodes and songs himself, letting his personality shine through in different ways. Since he loved jazz, he hired a talented jazz musician, Johnny Costa, to play the music. The red trolley car looked like the one he had ridden as a child in Pittsburgh. And he invited guests who reflected his own interests, from music to astronomy to the environment.

The puppet characters in Make-Believe also reflected parts of Fred's personality and the people closest to him.

King Friday

Lady Elaine Fairchilde

Daniel Tiger was sweet and gentle. King Friday XIII liked to be the person in charge. Fred felt that way sometimes, too! Lady Elaine Fairchilde was named for Fred's sister.

She was the mischief maker of Make-Believe and loved to joke around. And Queen Sara Saturday was a kind and wise person. Everyone knew her character was similar to Fred's wife, Joanne.

Queen Sara

Occasionally, Joanne and Fred's sons would appear on the show, but mostly Fred made sure his children grew up out of the spotlight. He wanted them to have normal childhoods. Someone once asked Fred's younger son, John, "What's it like to have Mister Rogers for a father?" John answered, "Well, he's the only father I ever had!"

For many other children, Fred was also like a father. They felt they could always count on him.

Johnny Costa (1922–1996)

Johnny Costa was born in Pennsylvania and learned to play the accordion by the time he was seven. By age ten, he was earning money performing at weddings and parties. In high school he mastered the piano, and he went on to earn a college degree in music.

Costa later became a well-known jazz pianist. He was the musical director and keyboardist on *Mister Rogers' Neighborhood* from the program's debut in 1968 until his death in 1996.

CHAPTER 7
A Close-Knit Community

Each show started the same way. As Fred sang the opening song, he took off his jacket and hung it in the closet. Then he put on a cardigan sweater (usually one his mother had knitted). Next he traded his dress shoes or loafers for a pair of sneakers.

He might talk about caring for a pet, recycling, or sharing. He also talked about things children might worry about. Did a haircut hurt? Nope. He got one to prove it. What about a shot at the doctor's office? Yes, but only for a moment. In one famous episode, Fred assured children they could not get sucked down the bathtub drain— they were too big to fit.

Fred also took field trips to interesting places, like a crayon factory or a mushroom farm. He made films of these trips and showed them on "Picture Picture," a picture frame in Mister Rogers's house that changed into a movie screen.

A visit to the Neighborhood of Make-Believe was always part of the program, too. The adventures of King Friday XIII, Queen Sara Saturday, and all the other puppets were always exciting for children. Fred thought kids needed both a little "real" and a little "pretend" in their lives.

Who Lives in the Neighborhood?

Hundreds of people and puppets appeared on *Mister Rogers' Neighborhood* over the years. Some lived in the "real" world, some stayed in the Neighborhood of Make-Believe, and some traveled back and forth.

Mr. McFeely, Officer Clemmons, Joe Negri, Betty Aberlin

PEOPLE:

Mr. McFeely: Named for Fred's real-life grandfather, Mr. McFeely worked for the Speedy Delivery Service and brought packages to Mister Rogers's house.

Officer Clemmons: In the real neighborhood, François

Clemmons ran a dance studio with his wife. He was a policeman in Make-Believe.

Joe Negri: Mr. Negri owned a music store in the real neighborhood and worked as a handyman in Make-Believe.

Betty Aberlin: Betty operated a local theater in the real neighborhood. In the Neighborhood of Make-Believe, she became Lady Aberlin, the king's niece.

PUPPETS:

King Friday XIII: The ruler in Make-Believe was born on Friday the thirteenth. He had a good heart but was terribly bossy.

Daniel Striped Tiger: A shy tiger who lived in a clock, Daniel was Fred's very first TV puppet character.

Lady Elaine Fairchilde: Lady Elaine ran a museum and could be a real troublemaker at times.

Henrietta Pussycat: Henrietta was shy but helpful. She could say only a few words in English. She said "meow" for everything else!

Fred always wanted to do what was best for his young audience. When he asked a question, he paused to let viewers think about the answer. Nothing that happened was very fast or zippy. When he first started doing the show, Fred flipped his shoes in the air as he was changing them. He stopped when he heard kids were copying him and bonking themselves on the head!

Children saw the same familiar people and places in each episode. Fred showed them how important it was to have a community of friends and neighbors. But he sometimes introduced kids to a bigger world.

One time he invited astronaut Al Worden to appear on the show. Worden had been a crew member on Apollo 15, a mission that went to the moon in 1971. He showed kids how to put on a spacesuit and described what it was like to orbit the moon.

In another episode, Fred went to the Soviet Union (now Russia), where he appeared on a similar children's program. At the time, the Soviet Union and the United States were in the middle of the Cold War. Both nations wanted to prevent the other from gaining too much power. Did that mean Soviet kids were bad or strange? Turns out, they weren't. They were a lot like children in the United States.

Mister Rogers Goes to Russia

An exchange takes the gentle TV host to a new neighborhood

Fred wanted children to look up to him as a reliable adult. He was always friendly but never too casual. At the end of each program, Mister Rogers sang again:

It's such a good feeling to know you're alive.
It's such a happy feeling:
You're growing inside.

The message was the same one his grandfather had told him years before: *You are special.* Fred believed that with all his heart. And the children who watched his show believed it, too.

CHAPTER 8
Tackling Tough Issues

"Do you poop?" Fred got used to answering that question. Kids asked it all the time. They also wanted to know things like how he got in and out of the TV set. Fred tried to answer everything honestly and directly.

He read every letter he got, and he always wrote back. Sometimes he sat up late at night with Joanne, and together they worked through the mail. It was slow going. They kept stopping to read the letters out loud to each other!

But Fred got a lot of new ideas for shows from those letters. There was nothing too small—or too big—for him to talk about.

Discussing difficult topics made some adults want to change the subject. Not Fred. He talked about war in 1968, when the United States was in a war in Vietnam, and again during the Gulf War with Iraq in the early 1990s. He also tackled divorce, reassuring children that it wasn't their fault if their parents split up. Fred knew children got sad, angry, and anxious, just like adults did. Talking things out usually made people feel better.

But Fred didn't always use words. Some things didn't need explaining—they just needed *doing*. One of the first people Fred added to the *Neighborhood* cast was an African American man named François Clemmons, who played a policeman. One hot afternoon, Mister Rogers had a wading pool set up in his backyard.

He invited Officer Clemmons to sit down and relax for a bit. They took off their shoes and socks and soaked their feet in the cool water together.

Not long before this show aired, it had been perfectly legal to prevent black people from sharing the same swimming pools or beaches with white people. That had only changed after the Civil Rights Act was passed in 1964. Some white people still looked down on African Americans, but Fred believed everyone should be treated the same. He didn't say a word about it, but he made it clear when he put his feet next to Officer Clemmons's in the pool.

The Civil Rights Movement

Even though slavery—the act of owning another person—was made illegal in 1865, black people still did not have many rights. In many places, African Americans could not vote or own houses. They could not attend the same schools as white people or use the same bathrooms.

During the civil rights movement of the 1950s and 1960s, African Americans joined together to protest this treatment. They held marches to demand equal rights. Some white people were angry about it, but many others supported the cause. The Civil Rights Act was passed in 1964. It guaranteed the same rights for all Americans.

Senator Robert Kennedy with Dr. Martin Luther King Jr.

In 1968, two very important American leaders were assassinated. One was Dr. Martin Luther King Jr., a leader in the civil rights movement. The other was Senator Robert Kennedy. He was the brother of President John F. Kennedy. Robert Kennedy had been running for president himself. Both King and Kennedy were killed because of their political beliefs. Fred knew kids were hearing a lot about the violence happening in their country. He worried about how they would handle it.

Fred stayed up all night to tape a special show about the death of Robert Kennedy. During the program, Lady Aberlin talked with Daniel Striped Tiger to explain what had happened, in the most gentle way that Fred could think of.

At the end of the episode, Fred spoke directly to parents: "I plead for your protection and support of your young children," he said. "There is just so much that a very young child can take."

Fred could not protect children from big problems like violence or death, but he tried to make these things less scary. When he was a child and something bad happened, Fred's mother had told him, "Look for the helpers. You will always find people who are helping."

That's what Fred was doing. And that's what he was teaching kids to do.

CHAPTER 9
A Powerful Voice

One day in 1969, Fred traveled to Washington, DC, to talk to a committee of US senators. At the time, public television received about $20 million per year from the government. President Richard Nixon had suggested cutting that amount in half to save money. That would be a huge loss for public television. Many programs would probably be canceled. It was not up to the president, though. Only Congress had the power to make that decision.

Fred was invited to speak to the Senate committee. Maybe he could help save the funding for public television. Fred was good at talking to kids about important issues, but could he work his magic on adults?

John O. Pastore

The senator in charge, John O. Pastore, was a gruff, no-nonsense person. For two days, he'd already listened to many different people speak. Fred hoped Senator Pastore would want to hear what he had to say, too. A lot depended on it.

Fred might have been nervous, but he did not let it show. He spoke about how violence on television worried him. Then he explained how he used his program to help children talk about their feelings. "I feel that if we in public television can only make it clear that feelings are mentionable and manageable, we will have done a great service," Fred said.

Senator Pastore listened closely. Fred's words were having a big effect on him. "I'm supposed to be a pretty tough guy," he said. "And this is the first time I've had goose bumps for the last two days." When Fred finished speaking, the senator said, "I think it's wonderful. Looks like you just earned the twenty million dollars."

Fred sat back in his chair and smiled. He was so relieved. He'd only talked to the committee for a few minutes, but it had been worth it! Now there would be enough money for him to keep making his program.

Fred believed he was doing important work on the *Neighborhood*. He was teaching lessons that would help kids become happy people. Sometimes they were very small lessons that didn't need much explaining. Once on the show, he buttoned his sweater wrong and it came out crooked. Rather than shout "Cut" and start over, Fred just laughed and fixed it on camera.

Mistakes were part of life—and so was fixing them. The most important lesson was making sure kids understood that they did not have to *do* anything special in order to *be* special. That came just by being themselves.

When he was asked why he devoted his life to children, Fred answered, "Well, the children become adults." He meant that when children grew up, they would remember their experiences from childhood. The things they learned as kids would determine how they acted as adults. Fred wanted to be sure he was sending positive messages to the children in his audience.

CHAPTER 10
His Honest Self

After a few years of making *Mister Rogers' Neighborhood*, Fred took a break to try a new project. He made a program for adults called *Old Friends . . . New Friends*. He liked talking to people who led interesting lives and did good work. Some of them were his friends. He thought other people would enjoy hearing their stories, too. On his new show, he interviewed musicians, artists, athletes, religious leaders, and even his own barber! Fred had not moved out of the "neighborhood" for good, though. He came back in 1979 to make new episodes.

It had been nearly thirty years since Fred had started in the television business at NBC. A lot had changed. There were more channels and more programs. Commercials that tried to sell toys and junk food to children were everywhere. Fred didn't like it. Sometimes he was asked to appear in commercials. He always said no. He wanted kids to trust him. Telling them to buy stuff wasn't the way to do that.

Burger King once invented a character that looked and acted a lot like Mister Rogers. He even wore a sweater and sneakers. Fred wasn't happy about having his personality tied so closely to an advertising character. He called the people at Burger King and asked them to stop running the commercials.

Fred didn't want his viewers to think that he would approve of the advertisements.

In 1981, Fred welcomed a ten-year-old boy named Jeff Erlanger onto the show. Jeff used a wheelchair to get around, and Fred asked him a lot of questions about it. He wanted viewers to understand that having a disability only made a person different on the outside. On the inside, they were like anyone else. Together, Jeff and Fred sang a song Fred had written, "It's You I Like." It was one of the most popular episodes ever.

Fred was always busy, and he kept to a strict schedule to make sure he could fit everything in. He got up at 5:30 a.m. to write letters, read the Bible, and go for a swim before work. He was in bed by 9:30 p.m. each night. He didn't smoke or drink alcohol, and he was also a vegetarian. For his whole adult life, he weighed exactly 143 pounds!

When they could get away, the Rogers family liked to spend time at their beach cottage in Nantucket, Massachusetts. It was named "The Crooked House" because of its funny shape. Fred loved the ocean, and he didn't care that there was no TV at the cottage. Apart from his own program, he didn't like TV very much, anyway.

In his personal life, Fred was just as friendly as he was on television. At parties, he took time to talk with other people's children. At Halloween, the Rogerses gave out full-size candy bars, not fun size. And no fruit!

Everyone who met Fred said the same thing: He was the same man off camera as he was on. "One of the greatest gifts you can give anybody is the gift of your honest self," Fred said. "I'm like you see me on the *Neighborhood*."

CHAPTER 11
Growing Up with Mister Rogers

The *Neighborhood* was aimed at children ages two to five, so most viewers only watched for a few years. By the 1980s, Fred's first generation of fans were grown up. Now he was invited to give speeches at high school and college graduations. People cheered and gave him standing ovations when he arrived. They didn't just remember Fred; they *loved* him.

He was still making new fans, too.

One afternoon, Fred was in New York City when it started to rain. Everyone grabbed a taxi, but Fred couldn't find one. He headed into a subway station to take the train instead. School had just let out, and the subway was crowded with children. They recognized Fred. Soon they were singing, "Won't you be my neighbor?" to him.

Fred even had a fan who was a gorilla! "Koko" was born in a zoo in California and had learned to communicate using sign language. Koko loved watching Mister Rogers on TV. When Fred went to meet her, Koko recognized him immediately. She took off his shoes, just like she'd seen him do on the show, and then she used sign language to signal "I love you."

By 1997, *Mister Rogers' Neighborhood* had become the longest-running children's program on television. It had been on the air for twenty-nine years! That year, Fred went to an awards ceremony for the Daytime Emmy Awards. These awards are given to people who work on shows such as children's programs, soap operas, and talk shows. Fred was going to receive a lifetime achievement award. It would honor the work he had done throughout his whole career.

When Fred's name was called, he went up on the stage to get his award. No one in the audience was ready for what came next. Instead of just giving a quick speech, Fred asked the audience a question. When they were children, who had made them feel special? Who had helped them? Fred wanted everyone to take a few moments to remember those people. "Ten seconds of silence," he said. "I'll watch the time."

An awards ceremony with hundreds of people is not usually perfectly quiet, but it was for the next ten seconds.

The Emmy Awards

Each year, the Emmy Awards are held to recognize the best programs, performers, and crew members in television. They are given out at a formal ceremony that—of course!—is broadcast on TV. There are separate categories for shows that air during primetime—the evening hours—and those that are broadcast during the day.

The word "Emmy" comes from "immy," which is a nickname for a type of light tube used in early television cameras.

Fred had a particularly proud moment in 1999 when he was chosen to join the Television Hall of Fame. It honors people who have made significant contributions to television. Fred was in the audience, waiting to be called up to the stage to receive his award, when he saw a man come onto the stage. Fred recognized him immediately! It was Jeff Erlanger, who had appeared on the show when he was a young boy almost twenty years earlier.

When Fred saw Jeff had come for a reunion, he leaped out of his seat and ran onto the stage to give him a hug. And Jeff told Fred, "It's you I like."

When Fred made friends, he kept them for life.

By 2000, Fred thought it was time for a change. Both his sons were married and had their own careers. Fred had been living in Pittsburgh and producing the *Neighborhood* at WQED for more than thirty years. He'd made almost nine hundred episodes. Now he was ready to say goodbye. He taped his last program and left the *Neighborhood* set for the last time. The final episode aired in 2001.

But even though *Neighborhood* had ended, Fred wasn't ready to retire. He began working on plans to open the Fred Rogers Center, located at Saint Vincent College in Fred's hometown of Latrobe. The center was established to study ways to help young children use television, digital media, and other types of technology.

Fred had made enormous contributions to American children during his long career. In 2002, President George W. Bush awarded Fred the Presidential Medal of Freedom. It is the most important award that a US citizen who is not in the military can receive.

Unfortunately, Fred only had a short time to enjoy this new stage of his life. In 2002, he was diagnosed with stomach cancer. After a brief stay in the hospital, Fred knew he wasn't going to get better. He went home and died there in February 2003, at age seventy-four. Joanne, his wife of more than fifty years, was with him.

Millions of people mourned Fred's death. And they did not forget him. The year he died, an asteroid was renamed "Misterrogers," to honor Fred's love of astronomy. A few years later, a sculptor made a statue of him tying his shoes. It went into a park in Pittsburgh. Another statue went up in the town of Latrobe. Fans also can remember Fred by visiting the Smithsonian Institution's National Museum of American History in Washington, DC. One of his famous sweaters—a red one—is sometimes displayed there.

The Smithsonian Institution

A British scientist, James Smithson, donated money to form the Smithsonian Institution, which was founded in 1846. It is dedicated to promoting the spread of knowledge. The Smithsonian is the largest group of museums in the world. It also has gardens and a zoo. The different museums explore topics including aviation, space exploration, natural science, American history, art, American Indian culture, and African American history. More than twenty million people visit the Smithsonian's museums each year!

Many people have wondered why a British man would give his fortune to start a museum in the United States, but it's a mystery. Smithson himself never said.

Fred Rogers also lives on through his television shows and characters. Public television stations ran reruns of his program regularly until 2008.

In 2012, *Daniel Tiger's Neighborhood*, an animated show, began airing. It stars the son of Fred's original Daniel Striped Tiger and is similar to the original *Neighborhood*.

In 2018, when *Mister Rogers' Neighborhood* turned fifty years old, people all over America

marked the milestone. A documentary—a nonfiction film about a person or event—was released about Fred's life, called *Won't You Be My Neighbor?* A movie about Fred's friendship with a journalist, titled

A Beautiful Day in the Neighborhood, began production that same year. Actor Tom Hanks was cast to play Fred. Contestants on the game show *Jeopardy!* answered trivia questions about the *Neighborhood*, and the US Postal Service put out a stamp with a picture of Mister Rogers posing with King Friday XIII.

Mister Rogers taught kids an important lesson, that everyone is special in their own way.

Whether he was talking about something silly
or serious, Fred had a talent for connecting with
children. With him, they were always safe, loved,
and welcome. His gift was to care for everyone,

no matter who they were. For that, he asked just one thing in return: Could they do the same?

Because that's what being a good neighbor is all about.

Timeline of Mister Rogers's Life

1928	Fred Rogers is born on March 20 in Latrobe, Pennsylvania
1946	Graduates from Latrobe High School
1951	Graduates from Rollins College
	Begins job at NBC in New York City
1952	Marries Joanne Byrd
1953	Starts job at public educational television station WQED in Pittsburgh, Pennsylvania, where he works on *The Children's Corner* television show
1962	Graduates from Pittsburgh Theological Seminary (formerly Western Theological Seminary)
1968	*Mister Rogers' Neighborhood* makes its national debut in the United States
1969	Testifies before a Senate committee to save funding for public television
1978	Makes a program for adults, *Old Friends . . . New Friends*
1984	Donates one of his sweaters to the Smithsonian Institution
1987	Visits the Soviet Union
1997	Receives Lifetime Achievement Emmy Award
	Mister Rogers' Neighborhood becomes longest-running children's TV program
1999	Inducted into the Television Hall of Fame
2002	Receives the Presidential Medal of Freedom
2003	Dies on February 27 in Pittsburgh, Pennsylvania

Timeline of the World

1929 — The US stock market crashes, sending the country into the Great Depression

1933 — The first drive-in movie theater in the United States opens in Camden, New Jersey

1941 — The United States enters World War II

1945 — Microwave cooking—and microwave popcorn—are invented

1951 — India approves a new constitution, becoming the world's largest democratic country

1957 — The Soviet Union becomes the first country to launch a spacecraft, named Sputnik

1964 — The Civil Rights Act is passed in the United States

1967 — The first Super Bowl is played in Los Angeles, California

1968 — Presidential candidate Robert F. Kennedy is assassinated in Los Angeles

1976 — The United States celebrates two hundred years of independence

1981 — Scientists identify the HIV virus, which can lead to AIDS

1991 — The World Wide Web becomes available to the public

1998 — The first Harry Potter book, *Harry Potter and the Sorcerer's Stone*, is released in the United States

2003 — The US space shuttle *Columbia* explodes upon returning to Earth, killing all seven astronauts onboard

Bibliography

*Books for young readers

Collins, Mark, and Margaret Mary Kimmel, eds. *Mister Rogers' Neighborhood: Children, Television, and Fred Rogers.* Pittsburgh: University of Pittsburgh Press, 1996.

*DiFranco, Joann, and Anthony DiFranco. *Mister Rogers: Good Neighbor to America's Children.* Minneapolis: Dillon Press, 1983.

Herman, Karen. Fred Rogers Interview. **The Television Academy Foundation.** July 22, 1999. https://interviews. televisionacademy.com/interviews/fred-rogers#about.

Kimmel, Margaret Mary, and Mark Collins. *The Wonder of It All: Fred Rogers and the Story of an Icon.* Latrobe, PA: Fred Rogers Center, September 2008. http://fredrogers143. wpengine.com/wp-content/uploads/2015/09/The-Wonder-of-It-All.pdf.

Laskas, Jeanne Marie. "The Good Life—and Works—of Mister Rogers." *Life.* November 1992.

Long, Michael G. *Peaceful Neighbor: Discovering the Countercultural Mister Rogers.* Louisville, KY: Westminster John Knox Press, 2015.

Rogers, Fred. *Life's Journeys According to Mister Rogers: Things to Remember Along the Way.* New York: Hyperion Books, 2005.

Rogers, Fred. *The World According to Mister Rogers: Important Things to Remember.* New York: Hyperion Books, 2003.

Sebak, Rick, writer and director. *Fred Rogers: America's Favorite Neighbor*, DVD video. Pittsburgh: Family Communications and WQED Multimedia. 2003.

Zoba, Wendy Murray. "Won't You Be My Neighbor?" *Christianity Today.* March 6, 2000.

Websites

www.neighborhoodarchive.com
www.fredrogerscenter.org

WHOHQ

YOUR HEADQUARTERS FOR HISTORY

Activities, Mad Libs, and sidesplitting jokes!
Discover the Who HQ books beyond the biographies

Who? What? Where?

Learn more at whohq.com!